Survival Family Basics

The Prepper's Survival Guide to Bugging Out When You Absolutely Positively Can't Stay There Any Longer

Macenzie Guiver

Macenzie Guiver

Just to say Thank You for Purchasing this Book I want to give you a gift <u>100% absolutely FREE</u>

A Copy of My Upcoming Special Report "The Prepper's Supplies Guide for When Disaster Strikes"

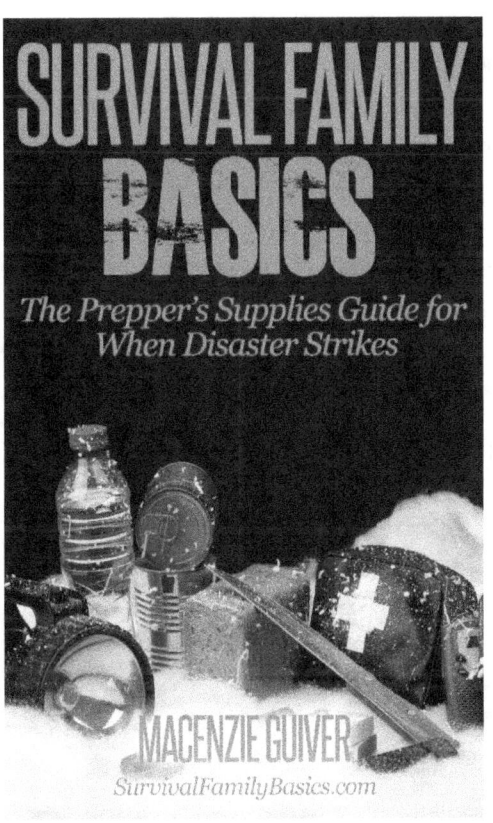

Go to <u>www.SurvivalFamilyBasics.com</u> to Sign Up to Receive Your FREE Gift

Table of Contents

Introduction

I want to thank you and congratulate you for purchasing the book, "***Survival Family Basics - The Prepper Survival Guide to Bugging Out When You Absolutely Positively Can't Stay There Any Longer***".

The last thing any parent ever wants to have to do is leave the safety and security of their home but when a disaster strikes, this is exactly what may be required in order to keep your family safe from harm. It is an unfortunate fact that no matter where you live, there is always the possibility that some kind of crisis will render your home or the area where you live unsafe.

From earthquakes to hurricanes to wildfires to terrorism, the list of possible disasters seems to get longer every day and the only logical way to respond is to prepare.   This is why I put this book together. The need to evacuate creates a greater logistical challenge than any other prepping scenario and for parents, the stakes are even higher. You might be able to go without food for a few days or be willing to risk drinking water that might make you sick, but my guess is that you aren't willing to put your kids in the same situation.

This book provides proven tips and strategies that will help you create a bug-out plan, assemble the supplies you will need, and practice bugging out so that everyone knows what needs to happen if the need arises.

From deciding your bug-out destination to creating an inventory system for your bug-out bag, this book provides you with the information and insight you need to get your family and your gear out of the house and on the move as quickly as possible when disaster strikes.

Thanks again for purchasing this book. I hope you enjoy it!

Macenzie Guiver

Preparing For Disasters – an Introduction
"Being prepared is the best defense against unpredictability."

The world around us is becoming increasingly volatile and the threat of a natural disaster or man-made crisis often feels imminent. For families, these conditions can create a constant source of anxiety.

While there are some parts of the country where not having a plan to bug-out is just crazy, the truth is that no one is safe. You may not live in an area where there are tornados or earthquakes but do you know where the closest chemical plant is? Are they running trains near your home that contain oil, natural gas, or toxic chemicals? What about nuclear plants or high-value terrorist targets? The only way you can protect your family it to have a plan and be ready to leave on a moment's notice.

Take a minute and consider what would happen if an earthquake hit near your home. We know from experience that earthquakes can cause major damage to infrastructure, quickly overwhelm emergency services, and render houses uninhabitable – all in a matter of minutes.

Let's pretend that an earthquake hit right now and caused massive damage to your home. How long would it take you to get everyone out of the house? How much time would you need to make sure you have the medication your child needs, enough formula for your baby, or the important documents like birth certificates, titles, deeds, and insurance policies you will need to make a new start?

And, where are you going to go?

Knowing the answers to these questions before you need to know them is why it is so crucial to have a bug-out plan and bug-out gear.

The best way to ensure your family will be safe and you will have the supplies and resources you need to survive the crisis and rebuild once it has passed is to take the time to create a plan, invest in the gear and supplies you will need in order to leave quickly, and run drills so that everyone knows what they need to do.

Benefits of Prepping to Bug Out

By their nature, emergency situations and disasters happen when we are not expecting them. This is why prepping ahead of time is so critical. When it comes to bugging out you need to consider things you don't normally have to take into account and assemble supplies that may not have a place in your everyday life. But not doing so will leave you unprepared and unable to do what needs to be done when the time comes to bug-out. Unlike other situations, you may not have time to weigh your options and create a plan on the fly once the crisis starts. You need to be ready to act and able to take care of yourself and your family in the immediate aftermath of the disaster.

In our everyday lives, we have the luxury of relying on local emergency services to help us when bad things happen. If someone is injured, a gas line breaks, or there is a fire, we simply call 911 and someone comes to fix the problem. But during times of crisis, emergency services are not always available. They may become overwhelmed by the influx of need caused by the crisis. They may have experienced their own losses and damage making it difficult for them to respond. They may not be able to get to where you are in order to help you.

Prepping, to some people, seems like an exercise for paranoid people. But I do not believe that prepping makes you paranoid or scared or any of those negative things. For me and my family, having a bug-out plan has provided only benefits including:

1.
2.   Taking preventative measures to be ready for emergency situations actually reduces anxiety and fear, especially for children.
3.   Preparing in advance for emergency situations can help to reduce the impact of those disasters physically, mentally, and emotionally.
4.   Advance preparation helps to reduce the kind of losses that can accompany these types of situations.
5.   Preparing in advance helps increase the likelihood that your family will survive and be able to recover from an emergency situation.

The time to plan your escape and assemble your supplies is now. Don't fall prey to the belief that nothing like that will ever happen to you. Sit down, create a plan, pull together your supplies, and then practice it with your family so that you know you are ready when disaster strikes.

Where Will You Go
"By failing to prepare you are preparing to fail." - *Ben Franklin*

If you read 10 different books on prepping, each one is likely to advocate for a different starting point in your bug-out planning process. They may jump right into building the perfect bug-out bag or talk about the vehicle you need or touch on any number of other important topics. However, until you answer this question, it is going to be very difficult to answer very many others. This is because what you need to take, what you need to drive, and even what you need to wear can all change based solely on where you are going.

Choosing Your Bug-Out Location

Here are some of the most common bug-out locations (BOLs) along with some reasons why you might choose that as your primary BOL and some reasons that it might not be the best fit for you.

Local Emergency Shelter

For many people, this is the first place they think of when they realize they cannot remain in their homes. These are the community shelters that are generally located in a school or other public building and are manned by community volunteers or members of the Red Cross. As a prepper, you may be thinking that this is the last place you want to go because there will be so many other people there. And for many people, these shelters are not the ideal destination for their BOL.

However, there is one circumstance where this might be the optimal BOL for your family. If anyone in your family, child, spouse, parent, who will be bugging out with you has a chronic medical condition that you do not feel confident in being able to treat, this may be the best place for you to go. These shelters may not be staffed by medical personnel but because of their central location and community support, it is more likely that you will be able to get medical care for your family member more quickly if you are at one of these emergency shelters.

You can determine the location of your local emergency shelter by contacting either the police or fire department that services the area where you live. If this is your plan, make sure you know the location of the closest 3 to 5 shelters so that you have options based on road closures, shelter capacity, and other factors.

Friends and Family

Many preppers choose the home of a friend or family member as their primary BOL which makes sense for several reasons. First, you will have shelter and access to supplies and resources. Second, you have those things and are in the company of people you already know and trust. Third, bugging out to someone else's home is a low cost alternative to other more expensive BOL options. Fourth, this can be the best BOL for children. By staying with someone they know in a place that is even slightly familiar, you can lessen the trauma of the entire event for your children.

If this is your primary BOL, you will want to have a discussion with the family members or friends that you will be staying with to ensure they are okay with you choosing their home for your BOL. Assuming they are, you might also want to discuss things like helping them to stockpile food and supplies ahead of time so that if you need to bug out there you aren't taxing what they have available for their family. You should also determine if there is anything specific that you need to bring with you. For example, your brother and his wife might be happy to have you bug-out to their house but since their home is very small and you have a big family, you all decide that you will bring camping gear with you and effectively camp out in their yard. Having these discussions ahead of time ensures you will never show up on someone's porch at 3 AM in the hopes that they will welcome you and your family inside.

The primary reason that this may not be the best bug-out location for your family is that you may not have any friends or family close-by who would be capable of or willing to host your family for an undetermined amount of time.

Campsite

Choosing a campground and essentially camping out is another possible BOL. The feasibility of this BOL will vary based on the crisis or disaster from which you are bugging out. If there is a chemical spill in your town, bugging out to a local camp ground isn't likely to be a good idea. However, in many circumstances, this kind of BOL can be perfect for prepping families. Most campgrounds have running water and bathroom facilities which makes cooking, cleaning, and hygiene easier to handle while you are bugging out. Additionally, with the right supplies, you could remain at a campground for a significant amount of time, assuming you had weather that was conducive to camping out.

There are some drawbacks to choosing a public campground as your BOL. First, it would be difficult to provide any kind of security and you would be an easy target for theft or attack. You could mitigate this risk by joining up with other prepping families to create a secure camp of sorts at the campground, but if you are on your own, you may not be able to provide the level of safety and security you need to protect your family. Second, depending on the source of the crisis, you may not be able to access camping areas local to you. They may be uninhabitable, full, or closed because of the disaster. Third, campground fees can be expensive and a prolonged stay may be cost prohibitive for your family.

Remote Location

If there is a prepper nirvana when it comes to having the perfect BOL, this is probably it. Being able to bug-out to a remote location will almost always be the ideal BOL for most prepping families, especially if that location comes with a livable structure and resources like running water.

However, bugging out to a remote location, specifically into the wilderness without a livable structure, is not something the majority of preppers should do. Surviving in the wilderness takes specialized training that takes years to accumulate. So unless you already have those skills and feel completely confident that you can provide for and protect your family in the wild, choosing this as your BOL should always be the very last resort.

Unfortunately, securing land in a remote area with a livable structure can be expensive and out of reach for most prepping families. This is the primary reason a remote BOL may not be the best BOL for your family.

Multiple BOLs

While you should always have a primary BOL that everyone in your family is familiar with, you should always include multiple BOLs in your bug-out plan. This provides you with the flexibility you need to choose a BOL that fits the disaster or crisis.

For example, pretend that your primary BOL is your brother's house 40 miles away. Disaster strikes and all the roads between your house and his are impassable. Since you will not be able to reach your primary BOL, you will need to divert to an alternate site. Knowing what the next best option is before you have to make that decision will ensure you make the right decision in the heat of the moment. For the most flexibility and optimal coverage, choose BOLs of varying types that are in different directions and that are different distances away. For example, your list of BOL options could look something like this:

1. Brother's House, 40 miles, East
2. Campground 1, 30 miles, West
3. Campground 2, 25 miles North
4. Sister's House, 75 miles, Southwest

Now that you know where you are going, you have some other decisions to make including, how you are going to get there.

How Will You Get There

The basis of your bug-out plan is your BOL and now that you have that, you can move on to the next most important question – how are you going to get there. While many preppers opt for a special vehicle specifically designed or equipped for bugging out called a bug-out vehicle (BOV), this is not necessary. But you do need to determine how you and your family will get from your home to your BOL.

Methods of Travel

Obviously, the preferred method of travel is always going to be in some kind of vehicle. The less human energy you need to get you from point A to point B, the less energy you will have to replace through the intake of calories. Additionally, traveling on foot is more time consuming and infinitely more dangerous that almost any other mode of transportation, especially during a disaster.

However, vehicular travel is not always possible depending on the circumstances of the crisis. The best way to be able to overcome this obstacle is to plan for it ahead of time. Here are some of the methods of travel you can use to bug-out and the pros and cons of each method.

Driving Your Family Vehicle

In most circumstances, this is going to be the optimal mode of travel. For starters, if you have small children, their car seats and safety restraints will generally already be appropriately installed in the vehicle. This can save minutes that can save lives. Using this as your primary vehicle also means you do not need to invest in a specialized BOV or keep it maintained, registered, and insured. This results in a significant savings that can be used toward more valuable preps.

Utilizing your family vehicle also means you will be driving a vehicle you are familiar with, which becomes more important in crisis or disaster situations. You are also more likely to keep the gas tank full which is crucial when you have to bug-out with little notice.

However, there are some important considerations that you need to weigh in deciding if this is your primary mode of bug-out transportation. First, you need to determine if you can you fit everyone and everything you need to take with you in the vehicle. Second, you need to decide if this vehicle will be able to drive over debris and roads that are less than perfect.

Driving a Bug-Out Vehicle

In some cases, procuring a BOV makes sense. If you have a large family and your family car cannot hold everyone and everything at the same time, it may make more sense to invest in something inexpensive that can provide the space you need. You might want to look into used RVs or even old school buses as potential BOVs.

If you live in a remote area or your BOL is in a remote area and you are concerned about being able to travel over debris covered or damaged roads, a BOV with all-terrain capabilities might be worth the investment.

Biking

Another alternative to traveling by foot is to travel by bicycle. This is a possibility that many preppers overlook. While it doesn't provide the protection and speed that a car does, it will require less energy than walking and it will decrease the time it will take you to get to your BOL.

This is only a good option if all family members are good bike riders and your BOL is close enough that the smallest child riding will be able to reach it with ease. Remember, you may not be able to make a straight shot on the day of the disaster. Road conditions may require you to take detours that lengthen your route. Making sure that your destination is easily reachable by the one with the smallest legs helps ensure you will be able to arrive at your destination.

You can also secure smaller children in bike seats that attach to the parents bike. Just make sure you take several trips like this when conditions are optimal so that you are very familiar with how the bike will handle with the extra weight.

Walking

Although it is often the way many preppers talk about bugging out, grabbing your pack and heading out on foot should actually be a last resort, especially if you have small children. Both walking and biking will actually require you to bring more equipment which means more weight in everyone's pack. Walking with small children in tow will limit the distance you can cover each day, meaning you could be traveling in the open, living outside, and completely unprotected from the elements and other people for as much as a week or more.

Because of the unpredictable nature of disasters, however, you need to have a plan in place in the event that you are required to walk. This may mean investing in a wagon for small children to ride in or buying a hard cart that you can use to help transport the extra equipment you will need without adding more weight to your pack.

Multiple Methods of Travel

Just like with your BOL, you will want to plan for a primary mode of transportation and several back-up options. In essence, you need to plan so that you can drive, bike, or walk because the circumstances that you find yourself in may dictate which options are actually available to you and which are not.

Planning ahead means you will know if you can fit everyone and everything in your family vehicle or if you need to plan to take two vehicles. It will ensure you have bikes and helmets for everyone that can ride and seats or buggies for those who can't. It will also ensure that you have the extra equipment you will need on hand if you have to bike or walk.
Now that you know where you are going and how you are going to get there, you have some other decisions to make including, what you will need to take for the trip.

What Do You Need to Take

When someone talks about taking things along when it is time to bug-out, they are referring to your bug-out bag (BOB). The purpose of this bag is to provide you with everything you need to survive for the first 72 hours. You need to be able to carry it, easily, because you may have to carry it with you while walking for long distances. For this reason, most BOBs are backpacks because you can carry more weight for longer periods of time without causing injury if you are carrying the weight on your back.

Who Needs a Bug-Out Bag

If you are a single adult or an adult couple, the answer is simple. You need one. Your spouse needs one. But when your bug-out plan includes children, the question can become a little more challenging to answer.

If you think back to the purpose of the BOB, it is obvious that children, regardless of their age, will need supplies in order to survive for three days. But that doesn't necessarily mean that you need to have BOBs for each child.

Additionally, what each child needs will differ by their age, but we will cover that in more detail later in this chapter. For now, here is an overview of bug-out bag information at each age/stage.

- Infants and Children Under 5 – Carrying a bug-out bag is not realistic, everything they need will need to be included in one of the other family members BOB.
- Children 6-10 – At this age, it depends on the child. Most children in this age group can carry a small BOB but the majority of the supplies you will need to care

for them will need to be included in another family member's BOB.

- Children age 12-15 – These children are old enough and generally big enough to carry their own full size BOB. However, you will need to make sure it is still lightweight enough for them to be able to manage. Depending on their size, some items may have to be carried in another family member's BOB.
- Children 16 and up – They should be able to carry as much as their parents and can often help take some of the load of the items needed for other children.

The decision of who in your family needs a bug-out bag has to be made based on your individual situation. However, the supplies you need to have in your combined BOBs must be enough to support all family members, regardless of how many bags you end up making.

What Goes in Your BOB

The decision of what to include or not include in your BOB is an individual choice which is why many of the "off-the-shelf" options don't end up being worth the money they cost. You need to consider the needs of you and any other individuals whose survival is based on what is in your bags. You also need to consider things like terrain, weather, and the distance you may have to travel. To help you decide what you will need to have in your BOB to survive, here is a fairly comprehensive list of the types of thing you might find in a BOB.

Water

Water is the most essential item in your BOB because of everything you will pack into that bag; it is the one thing you cannot live without.

In determining how much water to take with you, you need to consider how much water you can actually carry. One gallon of water weighs 8 pounds and ideally, you need three gallons per person to survive for 3 days. But is it realistic to carry almost 30 pounds of water with you? This is one place where having the water on hand to bring with you if you are in a vehicle is great as long as you have a way to procure more clean water while you are on the road if you end up having to walk.

First, decide how much water you can take with you in a car and on foot. Once you know those answers, you can look at the available alternatives for getting more water while you are on the move if you need it. Here are the basic water supplies that you may want to include in your BOB.

- Water – However much you can load if you are driving or carry if you are not.
- Water Bottle – This gives you an easy way to carry a small amount of water in an easy to reach location.
- Collapsible Water Bottle – These often hold 5 gallons and can offer extra storage capacity.
- Water Purification Systems – These are tools you can use to make water you find along the way and make it safe to drink. This is essential if you will be walking and cannot carry all the water you need.
- Water Filters – These are also tools that can render found water safe to drink.
- Water Purification Tablets – Another way to render water drinkable when you are on the move.

Food

Next, you need to determine what kind of food you are going to have in your BOB and how much of it you intend to include. There are many schools of thought on the right answers to these questions, but it is really something you need to determine for yourself. Just remember that if you are walking or biking you will be using significantly more calories than you usually do and you may need more calories than normal in order to replace the ones you are using up. Ideally, you want foods that do not require very much water and that don't need to be cooked. Here are some of the most common foods included in BOBs.

- Survival rations
- Protein/energy bars
- MREs
- Backpacking meals
- Beef jerky
- Oatmeal
- Nuts
- Tuna
- Dehydrated soup
- Granola bars
- Dried fruit
- Trail Mix

Cooking Kit

If you plan to bring any food that needs preparation, you will also need to include the following items in a cooking kit. Thankfully, with the exception of the first two, you won't need to include these items in every BOB; just one set will be enough for your whole family.

- Spork or other utensils
- Metal Cup
- Can Opener
- Metal Cooking Pot

- Pot Scrubber
- Portable Stove
- Stove Fuel

Clothing

When you consider what you will need to include for clothing in your BOB, try and keep in mind that you are bugging out, not going on vacation. This means you may not need three separate changes of clothes but you may want 5 pairs of socks. You also need to keep the different kinds of weather you may encounter in mind. If you live where the winter means cold and snow, you may need to swap out the clothes you keep in your BOB seasonally to ensure you have weather appropriate clothing.

Ideally, you need to have two complete sets of clothing so that you have dry clothes to change into if you get wet. Bugging out in wet clothes is uncomfortable and can also decrease the amount of time it takes for hypothermia to set in.

Determining the kinds of clothes you want to include is an individual decision. Here are some of the items of clothing you will commonly find in a BOB.

- Hiking Boots – a solid pair of boots are a must have regardless of how you are traveling. Make sure you waterproof them so that you have a better chance of keeping your feet dry.
- A pair of pants – Preferably not jeans, ideally made of material that wicks away water from the skin.
- 2 – 6 pairs of socks – Pick socks made for backpacking or hiking, generally not those made of cotton
- 2 pairs of underwear

- A long sleeve shirt
- A short sleeve shirt
- A waterproof jacket
- Long underwear
- A hat – can be a winter hat or a hat to keep the sun off your face depending on the season.
- A bandana
- A pair of sturdy work gloves
- Rain poncho and/or rain gear

First Aid Kit

Every BOB should have some basic first aid supplies and it is also a good idea to create one master kit that includes more items to include in one of your family's bags. What you choose to include or not include is a personal decision but this is one of those times that having more than you need is much better than not having the one thing you need. While this is not an exhaustive list, here are some of the most common items you will find in a BOB first aid kit.

- Daily medications – Don't rely on your adrenaline-soaked brain to remember to grab the medications your family needs every day on your way out the door. Get extra and keep them in your BOB.
- Band-aids, bandages, gauze, medical tape
- Butterfly closures
- Anti-bacterial cream
- Aspirin, ibuprofen
- Burn cream
- Hydrocortisone cream
- Diarrhea medication
- Antihistamines
- Antacids

- Sterile sutures
- Ace bandage
- Alcohol wipes
- Tweezers
- Cotton swabs and cotton balls
- Latex gloves
- thermometer
- Safety scissors

(For a more in-depth look at Emergency/Disaster First Aid and what you may need check out *Survival Family Basics – The Prepper's Emergency First Aid & Survival Medicine Handbook*)

Shelter

Your interim shelter needs will depend on your bug-out plan. This means that you may need more equipment if you are planning to walk than if you are planning to drive. However, if you choose not to include the shelter/camping/sleeping equipment you would need if you were bugging out on foot in your BOB, you may want to consider creating a separate bag or pack that contains these items in case you have to head off on foot contrary to your plan.

If you are in a vehicle, you can simply use the vehicle as your shelter if the need arises.

Here are some of the common items you might find in a BOB related to shelter and sleeping.

- Tent
- Tarp
- Sleeping bag
- Sleeping mat

- Hammock
- Wool blanket

Hygiene

This is one of the most overlooked categories when most preppers are putting together their BOB. Because of the relative safety of the world we live in, we don't often consider how critical proper hygiene is to our health. It doesn't take many days without running water for disease to get a foothold and begin spreading. Simple cuts can become life-threatening infections when we lack the ability to thoroughly wash our hands. The importance of following proper hygienic practices in disaster situations cannot be overstated. The purpose of the hygiene supplies included in your BOB is provide you with the necessary means to go to the bathroom, properly handle human waste, and thoroughly wash your hands. Common hygiene related items you will find in a BOB include:

- Toilet paper
- Small trash bags
- Soap
- Hand Sanitizer
- Deodorant
- Moist wipes or wet naps
- Toothbrush and Toothpaste
- Small hand towel

Basic Gear

In addition to providing for the basic necessities above, you will also need some other basic gear to form the foundation of your BOB. These items should be considered as crucial as most everything listed above except for water. Here are some of the most common types of basic gear you will find in a BOB.

- Waterproof matches
- Flint and steel
- Magnesium fire-starter
- Lighter
- Tinder
- Flashlight, preferably hand crank
- Survival knife
- Space blanket
- Duct tape
- Insect Repellant
- Sunscreen
- Important documents packet containing things like birth certificates, insurance policies, IDs, etc.

Miscellaneous Items

Once you have your foundation in place, there are some other items that you may or may not want to include in your BOB. These miscellaneous items are discretionary. For some people, they would just be extra weight, for others, vital supplies. Here is a list of common miscellaneous items that you can use to further build out your BOB.

- Sewing Kit
- 100 feet of paracord
- Paper and pencil
- Contractor garbage bags
- Binoculars
- Emergency whistle
- Resealable Bags in various sizes
- Dry bags

- N95 Face Mask
- Fishing Kit

Navigation

It is important to have the tools that you will need to navigate to your bug-out destination in your BOB. In an ideal scenario, the GPS service on your cell phone will be available to help you find alternate routes around impassable roads, emergency situations, or traffic jams. However, you cannot rely on that service being available. This means that you need a good, recent map of the area with all potential routes marked on it.

You should also include a compass, if you know how to use it. This is one of those items that can be as much a hindrance as a help if you aren't using it properly.

Communications

Again, optimally, you will be able to manage any necessary communications by using your cell phone but you cannot rely on it being available. This means you need alternative methods for communicating with the outside world. In addition to your cell phone, you should consider including the following in your BOB:

- Weather radio, solar and hand crank powered – as a bonus, many of these come equipped with a cell-phone jack enabling you to use the hand crank mechanism to charge your cell phone
- Solar charging unit for cell phone, GPS, and other electronics needed during the bug-out.
- Short-range walkie talkies – Can be used to communicate within your group as you travel.
- CB radio – Can be very beneficial if you are driving and cell phone service in unavailable.

Currency

As you think about everything required for your family to bug-out, currency may be the last thing on your mind. Unfortunately, that can leave you stranded with no way to access assistance or services. Depending on the type of disaster, you may find that your ability to access cash or credit is impaired. In these circumstances, both while you are bugging out and when you arrive at your BOL, having currency and items for trade can be essential in order to procure the supplies and services your family needs.
Here are some of the most common forms of currency you will find in a BOB:

- Cash, small bills only
- Quarters
- Gold or Silver coins

Tools

In addition to the other supplies and equipment listed here, there are also some tools that can be very beneficial during your bug-out. However, keep in mind that tools can be very heavy and when you are carrying everything on your back every ounce counts. Here are some of the most common tools you will find in a BOB:

- Multi-tool – This is like the Swiss Army knife of bug-out supplies
- Axe/Hatchet
- Foldable Saw
- Survival chainsaw
- Whetstone – beneficial for sharpening survival knives, axes, etc.
- Camp Shovel
- Machete

Weapons

This is always a controversial topic which means that the decision to include weapons in your BOB is one that only you can make. This decision should take into consideration your personal comfort with each type of weapon and the local laws allowing or prohibiting their use. However, for those preppers who do, here are some of the most common types of weapons you will find in a BOB:

- Handgun
- Ammunition
- Rifle
- Bow and arrows
- Crossbow and bolts
- Pepper spray
- Mace
- Tazer

While this list is overwhelming, remember that it is not necessary for you to include every single item discussed here. The most important thing is that you build a bug-out bag that suits your individual needs. There are very likely to be things that you decide you need that are not on this list, and that is okay too.

Now that you know what is going in your BOB, you have what you need to pick out the bag itself.

How to Pick the Right BOB

You may have expected this section to be at the beginning of this chapter, but it really belongs here because you should never pick out your bug-out bag until you know what you need to put in it. Otherwise, it is kind of like getting the cart before the horse.

At this point you might be wondering if you even need a bag based on your current bug-out plan. The answer is yes, and I don't even need to know what your plan currently includes. Remember, walking away from your house is always one of your bug-out options and if you don't make bug-out bags containing the supplies your family needs for the worst case scenario, you won't be ready to handle it when you need to. Even if your bug-out plan is to get everyone in the car, drive to your brother's, and live happily ever after on his stockpile of supplies, you still need BOBs in case a tree falls on your car, the roads are impassable, etc.

The first step is to figure out how many bags you will be creating. Once you know that, begin sorting out all of the items into separate piles for each bag. As soon as you have all the items for each bag in a pile, you can estimate how big the bag is going to need to be in order to accommodate all the items.

At this point, it is also a good idea to put all the items in a plastic shopping bag and determine how heavy they are when their weight is combined. Do this for each pile that will become its own BOB. You may find that one bag contains significantly more weight than the others because of the items included in it. Take this opportunity to move items between bags if you can to get each bag to the appropriate weight for the bag's owner.

Now take a rough measurement of the minimum area you will need to house all of the items for each bag. At this point, you will have a good idea of what size bag you need and it is time to start shopping.

In order to get the best bag for your budget, you need to know how much you have to spend. If you are creating several bags for your family, you may want to set higher budgets for the bags that will be carrying the most weight. Figure out how much you have to spend on each bag and then start looking.

You don't need a new fancy backpack in order to have a sturdy solid bug-out bag. Start your search at military surplus shops, thrift stores, Craigslist, and eBay. You may get lucky and find bags that will work perfectly for what you need at a very reasonable price.

If you can't find a great deal on a great pack, do your research before spending a bunch of money on something new. Take a visit to an outdoor sport shop or hiking store and try on the various packs until you find one that seems to be the right size for you and your stuff that is also comfortable to wear. Note the name and model and then search online to see if you can get it at a better price.

Don't get too stressed out about having to pick the "right" pack. Most preppers will go through several packs as their needs change, their skills grow, or they change their bug-out requirements. Find the best bag you can afford and don't waste time looking for something that is perfect or just right. Once you have your pack, create an inventory before you pack all of the items into your bag. This will help you keep track of what is in your bug-out bag and what needs to be added/replaced.

Special Considerations – Kids

When bugging out with children, you have a whole different set of needs to consider, plan for, and prepare to meet. Here is an overview of the special considerations you will need to take when you are planning to bug out with children by age group.

Babies and Infants

In essence, this includes any child that is still in diapers which are one of the first considerations. There is no perfect answer as to the best way to manage a baby in diapers when you have to bug-out. If you are traveling by car, the problem virtually disappears as you can pack whatever diapering supplies you have in your home in the car to take with you. However, if you will be traveling by bike or on foot, diapering is a unique challenge.

On one hand, you would be better off using old-fashioned cloth diapers because they are reusable which means you don't have to carry a bunch of them on your back. On the other hand, cloth diapers need to be cleaned and hung to dry which is going to take a lot of water and time you may not have.

On the other hand, how many diapers will you need for just the first three days and how much will they weigh? This is one of those decisions that you may have to make on the fly which means you should have the supplies you need to make the best of it either way on hand and ready to go.

The next special consideration for infants and babies (generally under age 1) is food. If the baby is breastfeeding, congratulations! Not only are you passing on valuable antibodies to your baby, you have also provided for all the food he or she will need during your bug-out. Just remember that you need more water and more calories than normal in order to produce enough milk.

If you are not breastfeeding, make sure you have enough formula and water in your bug-out supplies to provide for the baby's nutritional needs for at least the first 72 hours.
The third consideration is how you are going to transport them. If you are traveling by car, they should be riding in their car seat like they would at any other time. If you are walking, you may want to invest in a high quality baby carrier or sling so that you can carry them without having to actually carry them with your arms. You may have to forego carrying a bug-out bag if you will be carrying a baby so don't forget to take that into account in your overall planning.

Toddlers and Younger Children

Since these kiddos are too small to carry their own bag, you will need to make sure everything they need is being carried in someone else's bag. Make sure that all children who will be walking, even part of the time, have solid, study boots to wear, rain gear, and a waterproof jacket. Little ones can get cold faster than their parents and older siblings, especially if they are riding in a wagon or other conveyance rather than walking. Make sure you have warm gloves, a hat, and several pairs of warm, wool socks for each of your children.

As any parent will tell you, most kids are picky eaters and you don't want to kid yourself into thinking that your child's pickiness will suddenly disappear just because there is a crisis. The last thing you want is to be standing on the side of the road trying to convince your toddler to eat raw tuna from a can. For this reason, it is important to pack foods and snacks that they like and that they are comfortable eating.

You will also want to add the following to your bug-out master first-aid kit if you have small children in your family

- Children's Tylenol
- Children's cold medicine
- Children's cough medicine
- Children's anti-diarrhea medicine
- Children's stomach medicine

You can also pack small backpacks for children this size that contains comfort items and small snacks. Here are some ideas for items to include in small BOBs for your toddlers or young children.

- Hand crank flashlight
- Emergency whistle
- Extra socks
- Hat and gloves
- Stuffed animal
- A few small toys
- Trail mix
- Fruit snacks
- Granola bars

Older Children and Tweens

These children are capable of carrying at least some of their own supplies but in most cases, they will still need other family members to carry the majority of their supplies. This is also the age when you can get them more actively involved in preparedness activities like building their bug-out bag. This can be a fun activity for the family and it provides you with a great opportunity to being discussing the reasons why you are preparing in a non-threatening way. Here are some additional ideas for items to include in BOBs of older children and tweens:

- Flash light
- Emergency whistle
- Compass
- Small pocket knife
- Rain poncho
- Extra socks,
- A pair of gloves and knit hat
- Band aids & wipes
- Small bottle of hand sanitizer
- A few small toys
- A book
- A pack of playing cards
- A travel size game
- A baseball or small Nerf football
- Harmonica
- Bubble gum

Just keep in mind that even at this age, the BOB is not intended to provide the same things as an adult BOB. While children at this age may be able to carry some of their supplies, their BOB is really about providing some of the comforts of home and to make them feel like they are part of the adult team.

Regardless of the age of your child, any BOB you create for them needs to be customized for their age, size, likes, dislikes, and overall fitness level.

Finalizing Your Plan

You now have all the pieces to create you family's bug-out plan. This means that in a disaster situation, if it becomes necessary to leave your home for safety reasons, you will now be prepared to do so in a way that ensures your family's needs will be taken care of while you are traveling. Once you have finalized your plan and built out your BOBs, you should be ready to leave the house in a matter of minutes and have everything you need to survive for at least three days.

To reiterate, here are some of the most important things you need to take into account and consider as you finalize your plan.

- Determine your primary and secondary bug-out locations
- Learn multiple routes to each of these locations
- Find out where your local emergency shelter is and what restrictions they have
- Talk to your family about the possibility of having to bug-out
- Find out the process your children's school will use if they need to evacuate
- Assemble your bug-out bags and keep them in an easy to reach location
- Keep at least a half tank of gas in your car at all times
- Make sure everyone in the family has a pair of sturdy boots to wear in case you have to bug-out
- Be prepared to bug-out using different methods of transportation
- Practice bugging out with your family

Running a Drill

Now that you have your plan, your supplies, and your equipment, it is time to put it all to the test. Running a bug-out drill is one of the best ways to get your family ready to leave the house in a hurry if the need ever arises. It also gives you the chance to figure out how much time it will take to get everyone and everything out of the house in a real emergency. The best way to run this kind of drill is to bug-out to one of your bug-out locations, like a campground with only the supplies you have included in your bug-out bags and possibly a shelter kit. Even an overnight camping trip will help you figure out what items are missing, what things you might not need, and what things you need to change about your plan and your supplies so that when disaster strikes for real, you will be ready.

Conclusion

There is simply no way to know when a disaster will strike or the impact it will have on your life. You might be in the path of a powerful hurricane or have your home threatened by a wildfire. The only thing you can do is be prepared to get your family out of the house and on the way to safety as quickly as possible.

With the right plan in place and bug-out bags stocked with just the right supplies to meet the needs of your family, you will have everything you need to bug-out to a safer location. This is why it is so important to create a bug out plan, assemble all the supplies and equipment you will need to bug-out, and run a bug-out drill with your family. Remember, the primary goals in developing your bug-out plan are:

1. To ensure you can get everyone and everything you need out of the house and on the road in a matter of minutes.
2. To ensure you have the supplies, equipment, and tools to take care of your family's basic needs for at least three days.
3. To bug-out to a location that is far enough away from the crisis to offer a safe haven.
4. To plan for multiple bug-out locations, multiple methods of transportation, and multiple routes to get where you need to go so that you have maximum flexibility to respond to changing conditions in a crisis situation.
5. To develop the skills you and your family will need to bug-out safely and effectively.

By following the process laid out here for creating a bug-out plan and assembling your bug-out supplies, you are taking action to ensure your family has everything they need to access their safety net when disaster strikes.

Stay Safe!

Macenzie

Check out these other *Survival Family Basics* Titles...

http://www.amazon.com/dp/B00HG7Y4YS

http://www.amazon.com/dp/B00HYQ55W6

http://www.amazon.com/dp/B00I90UPSK

http://www.amazon.com/dp/B00J1VGJXG